500 JAZZ LICKS
FOR ALL INSTRUMENTS

BY BRENT VAARTSTRA

ISBN 978-1-4950-1181-8

HAL•LEONARD®
CORPORATION
7777 W. BLUEMOUND RD. P.O. BOX 13819 MILWAUKEE, WI 53213

In Australia Contact:
Hal Leonard Australia Pty. Ltd.
4 Lentara Court
Cheltenham, Victoria, 3192 Australia
Email: ausadmin@halleonard.com.au

Visit Hal Leonard Online at
www.halleonard.com

CONTENTS

PREFACE

I'm sure you've heard it said that music is a language, and it's true. Music is a creative form of communication. It is a means by which to express ideas, thoughts, and feelings. Think about your daily encounters with other people – bumping into a friend on the street, interacting with a work colleague, dinner with your family, or talking with your teachers at school. During these meetings, do you plan every single word, every single sentence you are going to say? Of course not. You probably come into a conversation with an idea of what you want to convey and improvise the rest. You can't possibly know for sure what the other person will say back, what distractions might come up, or how your environment might change. And what if your fellow communicator doesn't speak your native language? I battled with this in my months abroad in Peru and Greece. I was unable to share conversations at the dinner table, or to express my feelings effectively. My poor communication led me to catching the wrong buses to the wrong towns and I felt like I was always in the dark. I felt imprisoned by the English language.

Jazz is a style of music that embodies every essence of language. It's centered on improvisation and interaction. It's a social music. To understand jazz, it must be listened to, read, practiced, and spoken with other fluent speakers. It's thick with history and tradition, yet vibrant with new dialects and interpretations.

500 Jazz Licks is a book that aims to assist you on your journey to play this music fluently. These short phrases and ideas we call "licks" will help you understand how to navigate the common chords and chord progressions you will encounter. Adding this vocabulary to your arsenal will send you down the right path and improve your jazz playing.

My desire is that this book will serve as a useful tool to help you better understand the language of jazz. I sincerely hope you enjoy it, and wish you success in all your musical endeavors.

– Brent Vaartstra

HOW TO USE THIS BOOK

This book is divided into three important sections: Jazz Chords; Common Chord Progressions; Common Jazz Standard Progressions.

Jazz Chords

Here you'll find licks over chords essential to the construction of common chord progressions in the jazz idiom. It can be helpful to study these chords individually before bringing them into context. This section lays out a variety of ideas to play over major 7th, minor 7th, dominant 7th, minor 7th utilizing the Dorian mode, and major 7(♭5) chords utilizing the Lydian mode. Occasionally, a lick might include an extension to the chord, such as a V7#11.

Common Chord Progressions

The licks in this sections are played over chord progressions often found in jazz repertoire. This section lays out ideas to play over ii–V–I, ii–V–i (minor), I–VI–ii–V–I, i–vi–ii–V–i (minor) and I7–IV7–I7 chord progressions. These licks will help develop good voice-leading and show how these chords are connected together. Some licks in this section might stray from the original progression and outline a common substitution jazz musicians may utilize. For example, instead of playing a ii–V–I (Dm7–G7–Cmaj7), a tritone substitution can be used (Dm7–D♭7–Cmaj7). It's important to understand some of these substitutions and how they are applied to their associated chord progressions.

Common Jazz Standard Progressions

These are licks that are applied to entire forms of popular jazz standards. Every four bars are individual licks that focus on unique chord progressions within each tune. All the licks were composed to flow together musically, so you can play each lick individually or apply them to the next. This section will help you see how licks can be applied in the context of an entire tune, which is incredibly important. It also covers unique chord progressions not addressed in the Common Chord Progressions section.

Use this book like you would a dictionary or a thesaurus. It's not meant to be read front to back, but rather referenced according to your needs. These licks were written to inspire different melodic, harmonic, and rhythmic ideas. Some originate from the bebop language and other jazz styles, while others focus on patterns and rhythmic variations.

All the categories of licks are written in four different common keys. The primary reason for this is to encourage practicing them in different keys, and preferably all 12 keys. Find a lick you particularly like and work on it in different keys, octaves, and tempos. Practice the lick with straight-eighths, various styles of swing-eighths, and at different dynamics. Add expressive markings that lend an expressive, colorful shape. Play it over and over again so that it sinks deep into your conscience. Try making variations of your own and, most importantly, feel free to be creative.

Jazz Chords
Major 7th Chords

Minor 7th Chords

Dominant 7th Chords

Minor 7th Chords (Dorian)

Major 7♭5 Chords (Lydian)

Common Chord Progressions
ii–V–I

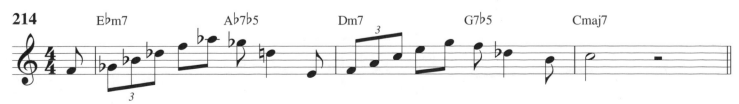

ii–V–i

I–VI–ii–V–I

i–vi–ii–V–i

I7—IV7—I7

Common Jazz Standard Progressions
Everything You Are Not

Ugly Dove

I've Never Met Miss Jones

Lovers No More

Oreo

Sudden Appearance

Solar Eclipse

Alto Madness

There Will Always Be Another Tune

Do You Know What Love Is?

ACKNOWLEDGMENTS

I would like to thank all of folks at Hal Leonard, particularly Jeff Schroedl, for giving me the opportunity to write this book. Thanks to my family, who have always stood behind me in my musical endeavors. Special thanks goes to my wife Philippia for her unyielding support and encouragement.

ABOUT THE AUTHOR

Brent Vaartstra is a jazz guitarist, teacher, composer, and writer who lives and works in New York City. He plays in a variety of groups in the New York metropolitan area and beyond. Brent has studied with internationally renowned jazz musicians and educators Vic Juris, Steve Cardenas, Peter Bernstein, Dave Peterson, Scott Reeves, and with composer and arranger Mike Holober. He teaches in the greater New York area and abroad through Skype.

To learn more about Brent, visit www.brentvaartstra.com.

JAZZ INSTRUCTION & IMPROVISATION

BOOKS FOR ALL INSTRUMENTS FROM HAL LEONARD

500 JAZZ LICKS
by Brent Vaartstra

This book aims to assist you on your journey to play jazz fluently. These short phrases and ideas we call "licks" will help you understand how to navigate the common chords and chord progressions you will encounter. Adding this vocabulary to your arsenal will send you down the right path and improve your jazz playing, regardless of your instrument.

00142384 .... $16.99

1001 JAZZ LICKS
by Jack Shneidman
Cherry Lane Music

This book presents 1,001 melodic gems played over dozens of the most important chord progressions heard in jazz. This is the ideal book for beginners seeking a well-organized, easy-to-follow encyclopedia of jazz vocabulary, as well as professionals who want to take their knowledge of the jazz language to new heights.

02500133 .... $14.99

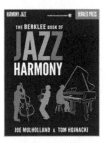

THE BERKLEE BOOK OF JAZZ HARMONY
by Joe Mulholland & Tom Hojnacki

Learn jazz harmony, as taught at Berklee College of Music. This text provides a strong foundation in harmonic principles, supporting further study in jazz composition, arranging, and improvisation. It covers basic chord types and their tensions, with practical demonstrations of how they are used in characteristic jazz contexts and an accompanying recording that lets you hear how they can be applied.

00113755 Book/Online Audio..................... $19.99

BUILDING A JAZZ VOCABULARY
By Mike Steinel

A valuable resource for learning the basics of jazz from Mike Steinel of the University of North Texas. It covers: the basics of jazz • how to build effective solos • a comprehensive practice routine • and a jazz vocabulary of the masters.

00849911 .... $19.99

COMPREHENSIVE TECHNIQUE FOR JAZZ MUSICIANS
2ND EDITION

by Bert Ligon
Houston Publishing

An incredible presentation of the most practical exercises an aspiring jazz student could want. All are logically interwoven with fine "real world" examples from jazz to classical. This book is an essential anthology of technical, compositional, and theoretical exercises, with lots of musical examples.

00030455 .... $34.99

EAR TRAINING
by Keith Wyatt,
Carl Schroeder and Joe Elliott
Musicians Institute Press

Covers: basic pitch matching • singing major and minor scales • identifying intervals • transcribing melodies and rhythm • identifying chords and progressions • seventh chords and the blues • modal interchange, chromaticism, modulation • and more.

00695198 Book/Online Audio..................... $24.99

EXERCISES AND ETUDES FOR THE JAZZ INSTRUMENTALIST
by J.J. Johnson

Designed as study material and playable by any instrument, these pieces run the gamut of the jazz experience, featuring common and uncommon time signatures and keys, and styles from ballads to funk. They are progressively graded so that both beginners and professionals will be challenged by the demands of this wonderful music.

00842018 Bass Clef Edition $19.99
00842042 Treble Clef Edition $16.95

HOW TO PLAY FROM A REAL BOOK
by Robert Rawlins

Explore, understand, and perform the songs in real books with the techniques in this book. Learn how to analyze the form and harmonic structure, insert an introduction, interpret the melody, improvise on the chords, construct bass lines, voice the chords, add substitutions, and more. It addresses many aspects of solo and small band performance that can improve your own playing and your understanding of what others are doing around you.

00312097 .... $19.99

JAZZ DUETS
ETUDES FOR PHRASING AND ARTICULATION
by Richard Lowell
Berklee Press

With these 27 duets in jazz and jazz-influenced styles, you will learn how to improve your ear, sense of timing, phrasing, and your facility in bringing theoretical principles into musical expression. Covers: jazz staccato & legato • scales, modes & harmonies • phrasing within and between measures • swing feel • and more.

00302151 .... $14.99

JAZZ THEORY & WORKBOOK
by Lilian Dericq &
Étienne Guéreau

Designed for all instrumentalists, this book teaches how jazz standards are constructed. It is also a great resource for arrangers and composers seeking new writing tools. While some of the musical examples are pianistic, this book is not exclusively for keyboard players.

00159022 .... $19.99

JAZZ THEORY RESOURCES
by Bert Ligon
Houston Publishing, Inc.

This is a jazz theory text in two volumes. **Volume 1 includes:** review of basic theory • rhythm in jazz performance • triadic generalization • diatonic harmonic progressions and analysis • substitutions and turnarounds • and more. **Volume 2 includes:** modes and modal frameworks • quartal harmony • extended tertian structures and triadic superimposition • pentatonic applications • coloring "outside" the lines and beyond • and more.

00030458 Volume 1 .... $39.99
00030459 Volume 2 .... $32.99

JAZZOLOGY
THE ENCYCLOPEDIA OF JAZZ THEORY FOR ALL MUSICIANS
by Robert Rawlins and
Nor Eddine Bahha

This comprehensive resource covers a variety of jazz topics, for beginners and pros of any instrument. The book serves as an encyclopedia for reference, a thorough methodology for the student, and a workbook for the classroom.

00311167 .... $24.99

MODALOGY
SCALES, MODES & CHORDS: THE PRIMORDIAL BUILDING BLOCKS OF MUSIC
by Jeff Brent with Schell Barkley

Primarily a music theory reference, this book presents a unique perspective on the origins, interlocking aspects, and usage of the most common scales and modes in occidental music. Anyone wishing to seriously explore the realms of scales, modes, and their real-world functions will find the most important issues dealt with in meticulous detail within these pages.

00312274 .... $24.99

THE SOURCE
THE DICTIONARY OF CONTEMPORARY AND TRADITIONAL SCALES
by Steve Barta

This book serves as an informative guide for people who are looking for good, solid information regarding scales, chords, and how they work together. It provides right and left hand fingerings for scales, chords, and complete inversions. Includes over 20 different scales, each written in all 12 keys.

00240885 .... $19.99

HAL•LEONARD®
www.halleonard.com

The Best-Selling Jazz Book of All Time Is Now Legal!

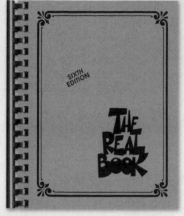

The Real Books are the most popular jazz books of all time. Since the 1970s, musicians have trusted these volumes to get them through every gig, night after night. The problem is that the books were illegally produced and distributed, without any regard to copyright law, or royalties paid to the composers who created these musical masterpieces.

Hal Leonard is very proud to present the first legitimate and legal editions of these books ever produced. You won't even notice the difference, other than all the notorious errors being fixed: the covers and typeface look the same, the song lists are nearly identical, and the price for our edition is even cheaper than the originals!

Every conscientious musician will appreciate that these books are now produced accurately and ethically, benefitting the songwriters that we owe for some of the greatest tunes of all time!

VOLUME 1
00240221	C Edition	$39.99
00240224	B♭ Edition	$39.99
00240225	E♭ Edition	$39.99
00240226	Bass Clef Edition	$39.99
00286389	F Edition	$39.99
00240292	C Edition 6 x 9	$35.00
00240339	B♭ Edition 6 x 9	$35.00
00147792	Bass Clef Edition 6 x 9	$35.00
00451087	C Edition on CD-ROM	$29.99
00200984	Online Backing Tracks: Selections	$45.00
00110604	Book/USB Flash Drive Backing Tracks Pack	$79.99
00110599	USB Flash Drive Only	$50.00

VOLUME 2
00240222	C Edition	$39.99
00240227	B♭ Edition	$39.99
00240228	E♭ Edition	$39.99
00240229	Bass Clef Edition	$39.99
00240293	C Edition 6 x 9	$35.00
00125900	B♭ Edition 6 x 9	$35.00
00451088	C Edition on CD-ROM	$30.99
00125900	The Real Book – Mini Edition	$35.00
00204126	Backing Tracks on USB Flash Drive	$50.00
00204131	C Edition – USB Flash Drive Pack	$79.99

VOLUME 3
00240233	C Edition	$39.99
00240284	B♭ Edition	$39.99
00240285	E♭ Edition	$39.99
00240286	Bass Clef Edition	$39.99
00240338	C Edition 6 x 9	$35.00
00451089	C Edition on CD-ROM	$29.99

VOLUME 4
00240296	C Edition	$39.99
00103348	B♭ Edition	$39.99
00103349	E♭ Edition	$39.99
00103350	Bass Clef Edition	$39.99

VOLUME 5
00240349	C Edition	$39.99
00175278	B♭ Edition	$39.99
00175279	E♭ Edition	$39.99

VOLUME 6
00240534	C Edition	$39.99
00223637	E♭ Edition	$39.99

Also available:
00154230	The Real Bebop Book	$34.99
00240264	The Real Blues Book	$34.99
00310910	The Real Bluegrass Book	$35.00
00240223	The Real Broadway Book	$35.00
00240440	The Trane Book	$22.99
00125426	The Real Country Book	$39.99
00269721	The Real Miles Davis Book C Edition	$24.99
00269723	The Real Miles Davis Book B♭ Edition	$24.99
00240355	The Real Dixieland Book C Edition	$32.50
00294853	The Real Dixieland Book E♭ Edition	$35.00
00122335	The Real Dixieland Book B♭ Edition	$35.00
00240235	The Duke Ellington Real Book	$22.99
00240268	The Real Jazz Solos Book	$30.00
00240348	The Real Latin Book C Edition	$37.50
00127107	The Real Latin Book B♭ Edition	$35.00
00120809	The Pat Metheny Real Book C Edition	$27.50
00252119	The Pat Metheny Real Book B♭ Edition	$24.99
00240358	The Charlie Parker Real Book C Edition	$19.99
00275997	The Charlie Parker Real Book E♭ Edition	$19.99
00118324	The Real Pop Book – Vol. 1	$35.00
00240331	The Bud Powell Real Book	$19.99
00240437	The Real R&B Book C Edition	$39.99
00276590	The Real R&B Book B♭ Edition	$39.99
00240313	The Real Rock Book	$35.00
00240323	The Real Rock Book – Vol. 2	$35.00
00240359	The Real Tab Book	$32.50
00240317	The Real Worship Book	$29.99

THE REAL CHRISTMAS BOOK
00240306	C Edition	$32.50
00240345	B♭ Edition	$32.50
00240346	E♭ Edition	$35.00
00240347	Bass Clef Edition	$32.50
00240431	A-G CD Backing Tracks	$24.99
00240432	H-M CD Backing Tracks	$24.99
00240433	N-Y CD Backing Tracks	$24.99

THE REAL VOCAL BOOK
00240230	Volume 1 High Voice	$35.00
00240307	Volume 1 Low Voice	$35.00
00240231	Volume 2 High Voice	$35.00
00240308	Volume 2 Low Voice	$35.00
00240391	Volume 3 High Voice	$35.00
00240392	Volume 3 Low Voice	$35.00
00118318	Volume 4 High Voice	$35.00
00118319	Volume 4 Low Voice	$35.00

Complete song lists online at www.halleonard.com